Paul will be doing his work experience soon.

He will be working in a warehouse on the other side of town.

Today he is going to his interview.

He is meeting Mr Kemp at 9.30am.

Let's see how he gets on.

1

He meets Parveen at the bus station at a quarter to nine.

Paul hasn't a clue where the warehouse is, but Parveen knows.

She helps all the students with their work experience.

"This is our stop," says Parveen, "and that is the warehouse we are going to."

Paul takes a look round him. He's never been here before.

Everything looks very strange.

5

They find the entrance and walk in.

Paul spots a bell, and he rings it.

A woman comes to the window.

"Hello. How can I help you?" she says.

Paul looks at Parveen.

"Go on, Paul, *you* answer!" says Parveen.

"I've come for an interview with
Mr Kemp," says Paul.

"Please take a seat," says the woman.

"I'll let him know that you're here."

7

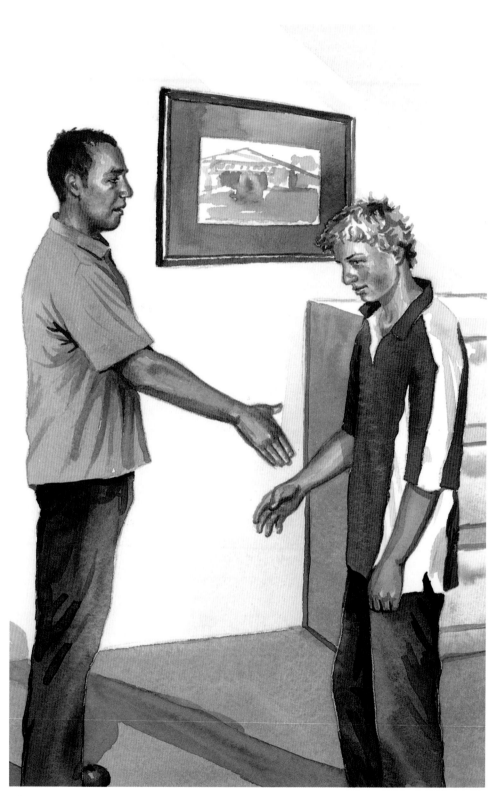

Paul and Parveen have to wait for a few minutes. Then the lady shows them to Mr Kemp's office.

"Hello! I'm Mr Kemp. I'm the manager here. You must be Paul and you must be Parveen. Come and sit down. Can I get you a drink? Tea? Coffee? A soft drink?"

"Oh… um… no, thanks," says Paul.

"No, thank you," says Parveen. "I have a bottle of water."

[A short play starts here. There are TWO parts – Paul and Mr Kemp.]

Mr Kemp: *Right, Paul, tell me something about yourself.*

Paul: *What sort of thing?*

Mr Kemp: *Well, which school do you go to?*

Paul: *Beech House.*

Mr Kemp: *How do you get on at Beech House?*

Paul: *It's OK, I suppose. I like some things.*

Mr Kemp: *What sort of things?*

Paul: *Well, I like Art and I like IT, but the other things are boring.*

Mr Kemp: *How do you get on with your teachers?*

Paul: *How do you mean...?*

Mr Kemp: *Do you behave yourself? Do you stay out of trouble?*

Paul: *Yeah, most of the time.*

Mr Kemp: *You will have to behave yourself here, Paul. All the time. OK?*

11

Mr Kemp: *So, you don't like school much. Let's talk about what you like to do at home.*

Paul: *Right, well...*

[Just then Paul's mobile phone starts to ring.]

Paul: *Matt? I'm in an interview. I can't talk now. I'll ring you later, OK?*
[To Mr Kemp] *I'm sorry about that... I'll switch it off.*

Mr Kemp: *That's all right, but we don't allow our staff to use their mobile phones at work. That's a rule. OK?*

Paul: *OK.*

UXBRIDGE COLLEGE
LEARNING CENTRE

Mr Kemp: *So... what do you like to do at home?*

Paul: *I like drawing and painting. I do a lot of that.*

Mr Kemp: *What sort of things, Paul?*

Paul: *I like to paint animals. We've got a cat, a dog and a budgie and I've done loads of pictures of them.*

Mr Kemp: *That sounds very good. What else do you like doing?*

Paul: *I go to the park with my younger brother. We take a football, and our dog comes too.*

Mr Kemp: *So, which park do you go to?*

Paul: *Springside Park.*

Mr Kemp: *I know it well. I used to go there a lot when I was a boy. There are some great conker trees there. Do you know the ones I mean?*

Paul: *Yeah! There were loads of conkers last year. Fantastic ones.*

Mr Kemp: *So when do you leave school, Paul?*

Paul: *I leave next year. Next July.*

Mr Kemp: *And what will you do then? Have you got any plans?*

Paul: *I'm not sure. I want a job.*

Mr Kemp: *What sort of job?*

What sort of job?

I'm not fussy.

Paul: *I don't know yet. I'm not fussy. I'll try anything.*

Mr Kemp: *Will you have any qualifications?*

Paul: *No, I'm no good at school work and exams.*

Mr Kemp: *You can get training at work. You should think about that. Let's go and see the warehouse now.*

Mr Kemp: *This is our warehouse. We store all kinds of gardening equipment here for shops and garden centres. We stock small things like garden spades, and big things like motor mowers.*

Paul: *Will I get a go on the fork-lift?*

Mr Kemp: *Not a chance! Sorry! You need training to drive one of those.*

Paul: *What will I be doing?*

UXBRIDGE COLLEGE
LEARNING CENTRE

Mr Kemp: *This is Tom. You will be watching what he does and helping him. There are lots of small jobs, such as putting barcode labels on the boxes, sweeping up and tidying, making the tea sometimes. Can you do that?*

Paul: *Yes, sure.*

Mr Kemp: *Well, I must get back to my office now. Tom will answer all your other questions. I'll see you after the holiday. OK?*

How well did Paul do?

What do you think Mr Kemp has learned about Paul? And what do you think Paul has learned about Mr Kemp and the warehouse?

Have you been to an interview?
Was it like this?